THOUGHTS
FROM THE
HEART

THE TREASURES OF TEACHING

ALYSSA JOHNSON

authorHOUSE®

AuthorHouse™
1663 Liberty Drive
Bloomington, IN 47403
www.authorhouse.com
Phone: 1 (800) 839-8640

Published by AuthorHouse 06/27/2017

ISBN: 978-1-5246-9783-9 (sc)
ISBN: 978-1-5246-9782-2 (e)

A Special Thanks to

Albert Pierre: Front Cover Illustrator

Glenroy Niles: Image Illustrator and Photographer who took the interior photo of the Joseph Gomez Elementary School

Gladys Niles: Image Illustrator

Jean -Louis Thomas - Photographer who took the photo of the Author

To my husband, Dylan Johnson Sr, my two children; Abigail and Dylan Jr, my loving parents Gladys and Allen Niles Sr, my two brothers Allen Niles Jr and Glenroy Niles, my Joseph Gomez School Family, my Community Baptist Church Family, Friends; and other fellow brothers and sisters in Christ, You were my motivation and inspiration for writing this book. Thank you all for always believing in me and encouraging me to express my poetic voice. I also thank you for encouraging me to step outside of the box and publish my poetry. It is because of you why I continue to write and I am eternally grateful. I truly thank God for you all.

MY TEACHING PHILOSOPHY WITH A TWIST

I must say that adaptability to change is a trait that every teacher must possess in order to endure in the race of education, but more so life. I say this because in 2012 my 10 month old daughter (Abigail Johnson) was diagnosed with a rear life threatening cancer of the eyes. I had to leave the job immediately. Upon return my class had been given away. I then became the school's acting Librarian. I also became a Substitute Teacher. Many people asked, when am I going to get my own class back and my response was God Knows best. I have learned as an Educator that one must make the best of what little they may have. I will teach and educate the students whether it is my own classroom or not. The ability to teach is not dependent on a classroom. It is something natural that occurs even when we are not aware. Students look at our lives and how we handle various situations. As an Educator, I have learned that just as I have had to adjust to change so will my students. It is my primary job to show them that yes change will come but the best way to handle change is to stay focused and positive regardless. I love teaching and yes at times it is overwhelming but the good always outweighs the bad. It is very rewarding and encouraging to see my past students and hear them say "You were one of my best teachers". It makes me proud because it just affirms that what a teacher does can indeed make or break a student. As an Educator, I am determined to be the best teacher and educator that I can be, because that will inspire my students to always be the best they can be. I now have my first grade class back and I can truly say that it has been AWESOME! We have embarked on a wonderful journey and my students have made me so proud. Yes there have been challenges along the way but overall both my class and I have learned so much. We are one happy family and the spirit of togetherness has indeed been evident. As an Educator it is my desire to continue instilling and equipping my students with the tools and knowledge needed to survive in this fast changing economy. As I said before, I love to teach and that is exactly what I intend to do.

CONTENTS

SECTION ONE

THE TREASURE OF BEING A TEACHER

THE REASON I TEACH

I've heard it all before

Why teach when you can do so much more

The Teaching Profession has no money

The working conditions are sad not funny

Yes it is true that being a teacher is not a piece of cake

But the reason I teach is for my student's sake

Being able to impart knowledge to little minds

It just leaves me speechless so many times

To watch a student move from step one to two

It just melts my heart this is true

The reason I teach is far greater than words could explain

It's a challenging profession but the fact still remains

That one's real reason for teaching must be an honest one

After all it does show when it is all said and done

I teach because I truly believe that I can make a difference in the life of a child

No matter if the journey is smooth, bumpy, or mild

The reason I teach is because I feel it's where I belong

I know it is not easy but with God's grace I am determined to be strong

I LEARNED FROM THE BEST

Who is that teacher as calm as can be?

Of Course it is Gladys Niles, affectionately known as my mommy

She is the best teacher in the world but you already knew

She is so creative and innovative; there is nothing she cannot do

As a child, I would keenly watch her as she taught her class

The room was never quiet, they always had a blast

Everyone wanted their child in Mrs. Niles class

That's because they knew that their child would have to give it their best to pass

One thing is for sure all students came out of her class knowing how to read

She would constantly integrate that phonetic foundation, this is true indeed

I always told myself that one day I would want to teach just like her

Though I am a teacher now I still can't touch her expertise, this is for sure

I just want to say Thank You mommy for being the best teacher you could be

Standing as an example for all to see

In my eyes you will always remain the best

For you always went above and beyond the rest

I have learned all I needed and I owe it all to you

Mommy even though you are retired now, we still see the teacher in you

WHO IS A TEACHER?

A Mother, Nurse, and Motivational Speaker

Here are a few ingredients that make up a teacher

Someone who can give a loving word or touch when it is needed

Someone who can clean a cut or even encourage students when they have or have not succeeded

Someone to listen to all what students have to say

Someone that puts the students first each and everyday

A teacher has to be willing to play so many roles

That is why a teacher is someone who must have a caring soul

Someone whose desire is our students to mold

A teacher is not just an ordinary person; they must possess a heart of gold

THANKS TO MY HUSBAND DYLAN JOHNSON FOR SUPPORTING ME

My teaching career has not been the easiest and smoothest one

It sure had some obstacles in it, just ask my husband

Many nights I would come home and just cry

I felt I could not go on; there was no need to even try

To be honest it was not because of my students why I was discouraged and had my doubts

But rather it was due to the unkind words and hurtful actions of some adults

Casting judgments and forming opinions before they even got to know me

My husband would say they are crazy not to see the extra ordinary teacher I would be

A teacher that has a passion to teach and goes the extra mile

A teacher that is not afraid to add her own creative and unique style

I thank my husband for always believing in me

Teaching me to keep going even though others at times may be unfriendly

Dylan, I say thank you for always speaking about God's calling on my life

I now know that it was worth all the tears, pain, and strife

For through it all you have encouraged me to give it my all, and stay a step above the rest

I Thank God for you, and throughout my teaching career I can say that I have been truly blest

VIRGIN ISLANDS TEACHER

V-Very unique and special

I-Intelligent and wise

R-Ready in every situation

G-Giving their all

I-Innovative and creative

N-Never backing down from a challenge

I-Investing in the lives of students

S-Sensitive to student needs

L-Loves every child

A-Approaching students with a positive mentality

N-Never letting the negative stop them

D- Daring to try different ways of teaching

S- Sharing their own experiences along the way

T-Talented beyond their years

E-Excited about what they do

A-Always willing to go the extra mile

C-Carefully molding lives

H-Helping students to strive

E-Encouraging those who need it

R-Rightfully deserving of all honor and praise

A TRIBUTE TO MY FELLOW TEACHERS

The life of a teacher is really something

Some days you don't even know what is in the horizon coming

You work so hard, you try your best

And little Suzie still had the nerve to get an F on the test

All day long you talk until your voice is gone

You try different ways of teaching; you wonder what else can be done

You want to give up but you stick it out

There is still that pride of being a teacher, what is that all about

It is true the race is not for the swift, but for those who endure

Teachers I give you applause and so much more

For each of you have gone above and beyond

You have taught many students right here in the Virgin Islands

Your past students are now accountants, doctors, lawyers, and teachers

Athletes, journalist, engineers, yes even preachers

My fellow teachers you have taught your students to be all they can be

You work really hard to ensure that they meet AYP

Teachers continue to give your all

You serve as an example to both big and small

You instill the knowledge needed to succeed

Your humble and kind touch will leave a lasting impression indeed

My Fellow Teachers, May God continue to strengthen, guide, and keep you

For his reward is the only one that matters when it is all over and through

A TEACHER'S TEMPORARY BLUES

Extra! Extra! You need to read all about this news

Have you heard about a little thing called a teacher's Temporary Blues?

Being a teacher can at times be very overwhelming

Certain days you don't even know if you're going or coming

For little Johnny came to school without his book and pen

When you ask him where they are, he carelessly replies "oh I forgot them"

And little Suzie just sits in the class all day and look

When you ask her answer to a question, you realized she never even opened her book

And Carl, my he doesn't come to school at all

When you ask him why he is always absent, he would say" oh I went with my mommy to the mall"

Day after day you deal with situation after situation

Then you begin questioning was this really my chosen profession

For being a teacher at times you get no public recognition

Just a pile of discouraging words and endless criticisms

But through it all these temporary blues do go away

For when Sarah says I love you, it just lightens the day

And when Albert begins to read, it just melts your heart

Because you know from the first day of school, he couldn't even pronounce the word cat from the start

And when Mary's mother says "Teacher I'm praying for you"

It fills your eyes with tears, because you know she understands what you are going through

So despite the bad days, the fears, and the tears

To be a teacher you have to be one who really cares

Not about the lack of supplies or the inadequate pay

Not even about the rudeness, or your fellow co-workers he say she say

For its all about the children not shortchanging them, is the real matter at hand

Teaching them to be all they can be and meeting their every demand

For when Tommy grows up and becomes the best doctor he can be

When he comes back home and sees you in the street, he would say "teacher thank you for believing in me"

So don't be discouraged your part as a teacher is very efficient

Say a little prayer sprinkle a little holy water because God's grace is always sufficient

So when you teach, teach to the best of your ability

And even if you reach just one life, that one life will forever think of you as a legacy

And when those temporary blues come back as they sometimes may

Just stand up straight look them in the face and say, my passion is to teach and I am here to stay

SECTION TWO

THE TREASURE OF TEACHING AT JOSEPH GOMEZ ELEMENTARY SCHOOL

FORTY YEARS OF EXCELLENCE

Hey what is going on over there?

Haven't you heard Joseph Gomez has made forty years

Forty years of Excellence and beating the odds

Forty years of faithfully serving others, Praise God!

At Joseph Gomez Education is seen as an important tool

Striving for Excellence is the golden rule

Many Administrators have come and gone

They have all paved the path we are set to walk on

They have set the direction that we must follow

They have equipped us with the tools that we need to face tomorrow

To our present Administrators Mrs. .Farrow, Mrs. Francois, and Dr. E;

We say hats off; and thank You for molding us into what we should be

We know the task you have is not an easy one

But we will reap the benefits when it is all said and done

To all our teachers we say take a stand

For your faithful dedication you truly deserve a hand

Your job is not easy but you still press on

We really do appreciate you for a job well done

To our paraprofessionals and office staff, we say great job on your behalf

For you to play a major role

You assist in developing our total mind, body, and soul

To our counselors you are both very dear

You help us discover our future careers

You listen to our problems and give us useful advice

You carefully guide us, you treat us oh so nice

Joseph Gomez has accomplished oh so much

Just look at our Track team, by others it cannot be touched

We have the most talented students all in one place

I know you have heard about our Superior performances at the District's Communication Arts Showcase

We have the best cheerleaders, pantomimers, and choirs too

Don't talk about our Band and steel band their music uplifts you
Our students are not afraid to be all they can be
We have no problem with meeting AYP
So we have made forty years go ahead and smile
We have persevered, and with perseverance we can go forty more miles
If we stick together we can always win it
There is no way to go but up, because the sky is the limit

THE NEW LIBRARIAN

As I came to school in August, I anxiously prepared my first grade class

I knew that this year would be even better than the last

In September, I greeted all the smiling faces

I marked each desk and showed everyone their places

I had no idea what was to be

In October, I thought my daughter would be quickly taken from me

I had to leave my class and get on a plane

I felt like I abandoned them, I felt a little ashamed

I knew I had to go, it was a matter of life or death

I could not see God's plan falling into place as yet

He was with me through out every uncertain step of the way

"I will never leave you," I could hear his loving voice say

His plan for my life was not clear

I returned to school in March, and my class was no longer there

They were there but they no longer belonged to me

God said "Do not fear, you just wait and see"

I heard whispers as I walked down the hall

Mrs. Johnson, you are the new librarian the students would call

At first I asked God, is this where I am supposed to be?

Some teachers were not very kind with what they said to me

But He confirmed; "My child I make no mistakes"

All things will work together for good, for my name sake

Every day the students ask "Do we have library today"

It makes me smile to see the role that I can play

For I had no idea that I would be the new librarian

But God is good, and he has used me as an inspiration

The students encourage me to give my best

God wants us to just trust him and let him do the rest

I am not quite sure what will become of me

But wherever I end up, I know that it is where God wants me to be

JOSEPH GOMEZ DAILY ROUTINE

We arrive at school and then we hear a bell ring

We must line up orderly and get ready to sing

We sing the Virgin Islands March and Say Our National Anthem so dear

Oh no! We could never forget to say the Lord's Prayer

We then recite our motto, "Schools are orderly places of learning and if we miss school we miss something new"

Then here comes Mrs. Hawley and Mrs. Stevens, they know exactly what to do

It's time for the word of the day and what will it be, will it be the word slaughtered? Or the word agony?

Next it's time for morning announcements then off to class,

We think Morning assembly is a blast!

A LASTING IMPRESSION

I can still clearly remember the first time we met

You were so cool, calm, and collective; though I did not know you yet

You sat and you carefully listened to what I had to say

And then you gave your wise words of advice; that just seem to lighten my day

They say a first impression should always be the best

I just knew from that first day, there was something different about you from all the rest

You would offer your assistance, no matter how much was on your plate

You never worried about anything, because in God you have Great! Faith

You would always say do your best because that is all you can do

Then I would smile to myself, because I knew what you said was true

You are like a second mother to everyone you meet

You have a loving personality that is always so kind and sweet

I know you don't like all the cameras or even being in the spotlight

But to let you leave without even a thanks, my heart just wouldn't feel right

I know that simple words could never show appreciation for all that you have done

But your heavenly father already knows how much stars to put on your crown

So as you leave remember that there will be some tears

But don't worry we cry because you deserve a galore of cheers

So farewell Mrs. Fraser and May you enjoy your retirement

We will never forget you, because your memory in our hearts will always remain permanent

A SWEET SPIRIT

Poem dedicated to Mr. Warner
Owner of the Breads and Cakes bakery in Wheatley Center St. Thomas
For his generosity towards the Joseph Gomez School for many years

For many years you have given with a smile

You desire no recognition; you just go the extra mile

You say it's your calling to give to those in need

Mr. Warner, you truly have a sweet spirit indeed

We admire you for always giving your best

When it comes to sincere hospitality you definitely pass the test

The world needs more people just like you

Never stop doing what you do

A mere thank you could never truly express the gratitude we feel

You have a heart of gold and you are the real deal

We thank you for giving back to the community

You are a role model for others to follow through out eternity

May you never grow tired in doing well

Because of you others will have a sweet story to tell

A story of someone who gave because his heart told him too

A story of a man who puts others first and himself out of view

May you always know, that here at Joseph Gomez we appreciate you so very much!

Mr. Warner you are the icing on the cake, you have that special touch

MY BERNE'S BUILDING FAMILY

Words could never truly express, what you ladies mean to me

God uses others to shape us into what we are supposed to be

Each of you have made my stay a very comfortable and encouraging one

I guess one can call you angels, when it is all said and done

You welcomed me with open arms, and treated me with care

You told me it would be alright and those words erased all my fears

I must admit that at times I wondered if this was where I was really supposed to be

The spirit of discouragement was trying to get the better of me

But at those times it seemed as if one of you would lighten the day, and showed how much you cared

Whether it was something you did or even one word that may have been said

It has not been the easiest experience being moved here and there

But God's promises are true and he will always be near

He knows just who to place in our lives to help us run life's long and tiresome race

God has a special blessing for each of you to embrace

Continue to uplift each other, and strengthen your special bond

We are not perfect but there will come a time when we will all need someone

Someone to lean on and cry if we must

Someone to share our joys and sorrows and in whom we can put our trust

Berne building ladies, may you continue to make a difference in the lives of those you may see

Combine your strengths and talents and together be all you can be

Thank you all for welcoming me

And letting me be a part of this wonderful Berne's building family

BIRTHDAY WISHES TO A WONDERFUL FRIEND

Dedicated to a Fellow Friend and Educator at Joseph Gomez

I wish you Happy Birthday and I say Thank You!

I truly cherish and appreciate all you do

Your friendship to me is the real deal

You don't stop being a friend because of a bad day; Friendship is not determined by how we may temporarily feel

Through your trials you still find the time to encourage me

This is definitely an inspiration most definitely

You are a good person and I know God will bless you beyond all measure

Ms. Thompson, continue to shine you are God's precious treasure

Don't let others try to get you down

Try to never let them see you with a frown

Because you and I know that God has our back

Once we keep our eyes on him we can overcome any attack

These things are just for a season

We both know that in time God will reveal his reason

So my friend press on regardless and have a wonderful day

I want you to know that I love you in each and every way

MY WISH TO YOU

Dedicated to the Teachers at Joseph Gomez Elementary
Christmas 2016

May this Christmas be a time to reflect

As you take time out to enjoy the many things, that at times you simply neglect

Like sleeping in late and not having to get up

Or maybe watching your favorite movie while you drink your hot chocolate, you know that big tall cup

Or what about taking that trip that has been put off over and over again

And buying that special something like a much needed appliance or that beautiful ring or chain

Whatever it is that you desire to do

My wish is that you just take some time out for you

Do something that makes you feel nice

Do something and this time don't worry about the price

I wish you all the best for this holiday season

Whatever you do, do it for love if that is your only reason

And always remember to treat yourself once in a while

We only have one life to live, it is best to face it with a smile

TWO TERRIFIC TEACHERS TOUCHING LIVES FOREVER

Well Well who would have thought that we would live to tell

The day these two special ladies would say goodbye: farewell

For you two ladies have earnestly taught with all your soul and might

Many times for the sake and wellbeing of the children you have had to put up a fight

For both of you have left a lasting mark on the Joseph Gomez School Family

Your faithful service and undying dedication has indeed labeled you a legacy

Mrs. Robles throughout the years your kindergarten classes has done oh so much

We cannot forget our 2013 Christmas program when they took us all to church

Your kind and tender touch is what each student needs

You gently guide and nurture them until on their own they are ready to succeed

Mrs. Dominique you never let your students settle for defeat

You diligently work with each child until all their work is complete

You faithfully support our students in the extracurricular activities as well

You have sincerely fallen in love with the steel pan and quadrille

So ladies I say Congrats! All the best!

You truly deserve the much needed rest

POSITIVE BEHAVIOR AT JOSEPH GOMEZ

Mighty Lions let's give a cheer

Because the Positive Behavior Initiative is here

We want to have Respect for All

Obey All Rules whether big or small

We will always try to Act Responsibly

Be the best that we can be

We are Ready to learn in all areas of the school

Having a Positive Behavior is COOL!

THE JOSEPH GOMEZ PRESTIGIOUS PANTOMIMERS

I started this group nine years ago

It has been a wonderful experience, this I know

To be able to express one's self in the art of mime

This unique ability just blesses my heart every time

To watch my first grade girls struggle just to stay on their feet

Getting disappointed, when at times their part they can't complete

But have no fear by second and third grade they are well on their way

It makes my heart so happy to see the maturity they begin to display

By the time they get to sixth grade, they change oh so much

They add their own unique style and special touch

It is at this point I realize, that they will soon leave and say good bye

Because they are off to Junior High

But to my delight some of them do come back to say hi

Then I smile and say "I'm proud of you and you are the reason why"

The reason why I gave up my lunch period everyday

The reason why you could not come to practice and play

The reason why I had to push you along even though you wanted to give up

The reason why joy fills my cup

I will continue to keep the Prestigious Pantomimers alive

It encourages me to be a mentor to my girls and always strive

I strive because I know not everyone will be academically inclined

Some may just embrace the Performing Arts and shine

A BLESSING

Encouraging Words to a Fellow Educator and Friend

Lately it appears that you have been a little down

You are a child of the king, no need for any frowns

The life of a believer is not an easy one

But God is always there to uplift us when it is all said and done

From the first time I met you I knew that you were not like the rest

No matter what others said, I knew you did your best

You are a great teacher and many of your students adore you

Why do you think God has not chosen another profession for you to do?

I have come to the point where I realize it is not about me

God uses our lives for others to see

Your students are watching and taking everything in

Because of you, maybe someday for Christ their souls you will win

Don't be depressed or give in

God's grace is sufficient, just rest on him

Well I hope you get a break for this Christmas season

Always remember Jesus is the reason!

Not just for Christmas but he is why we all do what we do

I am glad that I have found a friend in you

So may God richly bless you because you are a Blessing!

You can make it even if you think this is your season of testing

At the end you will come out as pure gold

God's promises have already been told

So cheer up, don't let anyone stress you out even me

You continue to let God use you, to be what he wants you to be

GIVE THANKS

Dedicated to my 2016 First Grade Class

I have been taught that in everything we should always be thankful

Well I give thanks for my wonderful class, they are so delightful

Though small in number they continue to amaze me from day to day

They are all unique and special in their own way

Brally, speaks no English but he is learning a few words along the way

It makes me smile when Mrs. Johnson he would say

It is definitely a struggle for him trying to get through

But I know that he will soon make leaps and bounds and show everyone what he can do

Chenniah, is full of energy and oh! How she can spread her wings like a dove

She enjoys being active and dancing is what she loves

She tries real hard and fixes her mistakes without making a fuss

Continue to be yourself that is just fine with us

Shalliqua, though small in body she is very outspoken

She is not afraid to voice her concerns and let you know when she is not joking

She gets so excited when it is time to learn something new

Continue to make mommy and daddy proud of you

Kayden, is quiet and tries to be as serious as he can be

When he is caught playing he smiles, he knows there is no fooling me

He continues to improve as the time goes by

One day he will spread to his fullest potential and fly

Yannickah, is my mommy while I am away from home

I get hugs all day long, as she says"Ms.Johnson, I don't like to leave you alone"

She is always praying that she does her work right

Continue to do your best, as you fight with all your might

Omari, has indeed come a long way

When he first entered the class he didn't have much to say

Now he is participating and trying as hard as he can

Don't worry I am confident that one day he will be a very successful young man

Kaylee, always has something she wants to share

In her own little way she shows that she cares

I know that she is taking small steps now but that is fine

One day you will be like the sun and shine

Amaiyah, is a little sweetheart, one in a dozen

She is so friendly and everyone is her cousin

She is a hard worker and she is determined not to quit

Continue to give it your all because you can do it

Oluwasheyi, is just as special and unique as her name

She is so expressive and creative, one day she will acquire much fame

Getting her work done is her most important order of the day

She makes me happy, what else can I say

Alexia, has the qualities of being a great leader some day

Not being bossy, but carefully taking time to guide others along the way

She takes pride in the duties and task set before her

Remain focused, one day you will be a star, I am sure

Jashawn, you are definitely one of a kind

You like to be a boss at times but this I don't mind

For getting your work done is so important to you

You will go far and make a lasting impression too

Anthony, you have great potential but you are a bit shy

At times you doubt yourself, I don't see why

Since the beginning of school you have shown progress

Do your best because you are on your way to success

Stanley, you are a very smart young man

You can do anything you put your mind to, of course you can

You try really hard and you never stop

One day you will be waving to us from the top

Brianna, you keep me on my toes

There is definitely no limit to what you know

You're always asking questions and this is a great quality

Never stop wanting to learn, make all your dreams a reality

Well there they are my wonderful class aren't they the best?

It is my smallest class in Fourteen years but I dare not protest

For every day they prove that they can be anything they desire

They make me laugh, cry, a bit mad at times; but all in all they inspire

They inspire me to be the best teacher I can be

They encourage me most definitely

I love them all so very much

They make teaching so much more enjoyable, and their eagerness to learn adds that smooth finishing touch

YOU CAN DO IT

**A Poem written to be said by Top Honor Students
at an Awards Day Ceremony**

It's not that hard, you just have to try

You Can Do It

Even though sometimes you may have to cry

You just need to believe in who you are

You can do it

You are a shining star

Don't listen to others, Focus on the task at hand

You can do it

Be bold and take a stand

Don't forget to thank others along the way

Like our parents

Please stand

Our Administrators

Please stand

And our teachers

Please stand

We love you, let's give them a hand

We never gave up that is the key

Just try and you will see

Just continue to do your very best

Study real hard for every test

We want you to know that perseverance is what brought us here today

Have faith in yourself that will carry you a long way

MR. LIBURD

A Tribute to a Former Principal at Joseph Gomez School

Humble, hardworking, dedicated, and oh! So comical

These are just a few of the qualities that describe our principal

A man who leads with great zeal and determination

Always keeping a leveled head and remaining calm in each and every situation

A good leader should serve others, is his life's creed

He always goes above and beyond to meet someone else's need

He does his task joyously, without looking for a reward

He then replies "I owe it all to my God"

For he has put God in full control of his life

Don't worry in due time God will give you your long awaited wife

On behalf of the Joseph Gomez school family, we would like to say Congrats Praise the Lord!

You truly deserve this prestigious honor Mr. Jamon Liburd

A TRIBUTE TO A DEDICATED LIBRARIAN

I have seen Librarians pass through the Joseph Gomez School

But I have never met one like you, so energetic and cool

I think being a Librarian is truly your calling from God

At times it might seem like you're not appreciated, But God has your reward

You make the students see that when you read a book it opens so many doors

You assure them that it takes them many places without even leaving our Virgin Islands' shores

How could some people not see?

The importance of the library

Mrs. Cruse never give up that fire and zeal

Continue to let our students know that the benefits of reading are real

I applaud you because you have inspired me

To continue to love what I do and be the best I can be

I thank you for all you do here at the Joseph Gomez School

Giving people their flowers while they are alive is a golden rule

PRINCIPAL EVANS

Dedicated to Principal: Avery Evans of the Joseph Gomez Elementary School

A firm exterior, with an I don't want any nonsense mentality

What you see is what you get; this is all a part of your individuality

You have served the world of Education for many years

There must be something that keeps you here, Could it be that you care

About the children and their best interest

I'm sure if you go back down memory lane, you will see the many lives in which you did invest

Ms. Evans, at times administrators get no appreciation

Just bad looks and lots of criticisms

As a teacher, I have learned that everyone has a good side

I have learned to focus more on that and find the beauty of others on the inside

Ms. Evans, may you know that you were placed here for a reason

May God strengthen you, this is your season

For I have seen that you are a diamond in disguise

Yes it is true, no need to be surprised

Always remember that everyone has a purpose here on earth

With God's grace may you fulfill yours, as he shows you your self-worth

ASSISTANT PRINCIPAL TYSON

Dedicated to Assistant Principal: Diana Tyson of the Joseph Gomez Elementary School

You carefully watch and then you make your assessment

Trying hard to keep a leveled head without making rash judgments

You take your time and say what you have to say

With the sole intention to keep the peace at the end of the day

Mrs. Tyson, you have a very understanding spirit and this is an excellent feature

Yes you are an Administrator but you were once a teacher

So I know you can understand the cries of teachers even deeper

You try to meet the needs of others the best way you can

You never think twice about giving a helping hand

Mrs. Tyson, when it comes to educating our students, you don't take it lightly

That's why they love you and think of you so highly

Mrs. Tyson, I could imagine that being an Administrator is not the easiest task

But thanks for showing the true you and not hiding behind a mask

Thank you for not being afraid to let us know when you don't know

It tells us you are down to earth and your human side it does show

For some Administrators act like they are high and mighty

Making teachers feel less important and more like a minority

Mrs. Tyson I wish you all the best for the years to come

I applaud you for all you have done

ASSISTANT PRINCIPAL SKELTON

Dedicated to Assistant Principal: Erma Skelton
of Joseph Gomez Elementary School

The new Assistant Principal was on her way, everyone was eager to see

We wondered what to expect; we wondered who this person could be

Ms. Skelton this may be your first year but it seems like you have been here for a while

You appear to fit in so well, you do everything with a touch of your Nevisian style

You are certainly not afraid to say what you have to say

Especially if it means supporting your teachers at the end of the day

You constantly share your many experiences in the world of education

Some good, some not so good but to me it has served as an inspiration

As you share one can see that you have had your ups and downs, but you never gave up

It shows that you hung in there for the children, and for this you deserve a gold cup

Many times as humans we judge a book by its cover

But when we spend time reading it, we soon discover

That everyone deserves a chance to make a first impression

Ms. Skelton, I applaud you for your boldness and dedication

May you continue to find new and creative ways to uplift the students and staff

I say a big Thank You on everyone's behalf

SO MUCH TALENT IN ONE PLACE

Joseph Gomez Elementary School is the place to be

Just take a look and you will see

Talented students of all sizes

So talented, winning all kinds of awards and prizes

Have you heard about our Girls Softball Team winning First place in the District?

Hats off to you and the team Ms Petersen, Because of the students' hard work and dedication they made it

At Joseph Gomez, some of our students can give Usain Bolt some serious competition

Thanks to Ms. Brathwaite and Ms .Joseph Our Girls Team won the first place title, and our Boys Team won 2nd place medals and commendations

The sweet music of our steel pan is so melodious, when you hear it, you want to dance

Mr. Sewer, we say thank you for believing in our students and giving them a chance

Give me an R, is what you can hear our cheer leaders say

Mrs. Donovan- Challenger. Your girls give their all, what else can one say

Mr. Charleswell, Saturday after Saturday you give up your time to work with the band

The students are sounding great; I see your future musicians, let's give them a hand

Here at Joseph Gomez, our students can sing too, Mrs. Carter and Mr. Barr, thank you for all you do

Mrs. Cornelius, you have the students singing with such harmony

No matter what class you use as a choir, they always sing such sweet melodies

Yes, we even have some skillful Artist around

Ms. Freeman, we won the T-shirt design another year in a row, I think our students are the best to be found

We can't forget Mrs. Charleswell and our basketball stars

They just made a 3 pointer, you know who you are

Well, what can I say, I am speechless

At Joseph Gomez, our students are truly blest

Blest with talent galore

I only mentioned a few, there is so much more

We must support our students in extracurricular activities

Who knows what they might one day inspire to be

For not all students will be a lawyer, engineer, doctor, teacher, or technician

We just might be molding our future artist, singers, dancers, athletes, musicians, oh what foreseen ambition

A HUMBLE HEART

Dedicated to Mrs. Hawley for receiving Teacher of the Year 2013

I would be ungrateful, if I did not take the time out to say

Mrs. Hawley, I truly love and appreciate you in each and every way

From the first time I met you, I knew that you were different

Your humble and caring nature was so evident

You always have a kind and encouraging word

You see the best in someone, no matter what truth or untruth you have heard

Your name is never caught up in any workplace confusion

You are an example of peacefulness; I have arrived at this conclusion

Mrs. Hawley I must say that your humble heart is the one quality that exceeds them all

You never complain, you are ready and willing to answer a beacon call

Your love for teaching shines bright as the sun

You never say "I don't want this student; you welcome each and every one

As a teacher you see the good in each child

You gently guide them, until after a while they are able to fly

Mrs. Hawley you have encouraged my heart so much

Sometimes your words are like a gentle touch

The touch I need to get me through the day

I once again say, I highly esteem you in every way

You truly deserve this honor and so much more

Your life has the favor of God: you are his child whom he truly adores

Continue to live your life as an example of how God can use and what he can do

You have your family, friends, students, and Joseph Gomez cheering and standing behind you

SCHOOL YEAR 2016/2017

What A Year!

At our Back to School Orientation, teachers were told that some expectations would be taken off their teacher expectation plates

Only to find out that was an irony, but wait

For this year the District has implemented so many new initiatives at the same time

It's only because of God's grace why I am not losing my mind

Introducing Anchor Standard number one

That's just the first one, I am far from done

Personalized learning is coming through the door

Make some room there is more in store

ECRI, is here to help build reading skills

I Ready Math is right behind, giving our students supplementary work and daily drills

In rolls one initiative, then another, and another

Sometimes I wonder which one they are referring to, Oh! Brother

But amidst the long list, the main purpose is our student learning to enhance

So I have decided to embrace these initiatives, and give them a chance

At times I wonder if teachers feel overwhelmed then what about the students whom we teach

They might be finding it difficult all these requirements to meet

Sometimes it is best to just master one skill and then move on

Than try to master a million and in the end not one skill has been learned

Well, we will see what will become of these new initiatives

By time we are finished, teachers won't need a plate; they're going to need a gigantic dish

PARENTS GET UP AND GET INVOLVED

Calling all parents of the Joseph Gomez Elementary School

It is time to get up and get involved, no time to look or act cool

Look at all the senseless killings all around

Open up your eyes and see what is going down

Don't just sit there and say it's not my child

Bullets don't have eyes when they are flying wild

Let your children know that they are a precious commodity

Together we can show them their true worth in society

Come to the school to find out how they are doing

Talk to them every day; ask them how they are feeling

Keep track of their academics and help them to choose a good career path

Let them know that they can be all that they can be, because they are smart

Stop letting them hang out on the street all night and all day

Let them know why they should make an honest living, show them the right way

Parents it is time to take full control

Children should act like children, not take over the parental role

It's not too late to save their lives

Just show them that you care and you will be surprised

Surprised to see the difference in a child's life once their parent is there

Parents get up and get involved, because another life could be spared

SECTION THREE

THE TREASURE OF MOLDING YOUNG MINDS

I CAN'T BELIEVE ABIGAIL IS IN KINDERGARTEN!

Eat your breakfast Abigail, it's time to go

My little Abby's off to kindergarten, I'm trying not to let my tears show

For I can clearly remember the day she was diagnosed with cancer

Questions about her future, no one had an answer

Will she live a normal life? Would life for her be very hard?

Today Abby is in kindergarten, I owe it all to my Great! God

For he created little Abby, and he knows his plans for her life

Though she went through some tough times, He was there watching over her through all the strife

Abby, loves school, and she is a little star

When walking through the halls, her name you would hear the students call

She loves to learn and she is as smart as can be

I have learned to never limit God and his miraculous abilities

She loves her teacher Mrs. Sewer; she thinks she is the best

Thank You Mrs. Sewer for your understanding and gentle touch, May you be truly blest

Well, I am truly grateful, that my little girl is growing up day by day

God is good; he works everything out in his own time and way

DYLAN JOHNSON JR: MOMMIES GENIUS

My son is an over comer, I must truly say

At about 1 years of age, he started speaking, and then he had a delay

The doctors wondered why he wasn't talking when he should be

It was alarming, but the reason we could not see

At times Dylan does and says things we cannot understand

But God will mold Dylan into what he wants, for we placed him in his hands

From kindergarten Dylan has never gotten less than a 93 percent GPA

I have learned not to listen to the diagnosis of others, because my God always has the final say

On the Smarter Balanced test, Dylan exceeded the standards of the school, district, territory, and state

I thank God for my son the genius, God is Great!

I know that in due time God will mold Dylan into what he wants him to be

I'll continue to trust and depend on him, I can't wait and see

WHAT IS BLACK HISTORY?

What is Black History? An anxious little boy cried

So many black people who wrongfully died

What is the true meaning of what happened back then?

Somebody please explain why did they kill all those innocent men and women

Well I think I know said a little girl, let me explain, let me try

I don't have all the answers but I'm told this is why

Why those men and women fought for what was right

They knew that blacks were not treated fairly; to them the whites were not polite

For Harriet Tubman led the slaves in the Underground Railroad

She too was a slave and wanted other slaves to be free; she did the best she could

And Martin Luther King fought because he wanted equality

For Black men and White men to live together in unity

Remember Rosa Parks, who never gave up her seat on the bus

She wanted blacks to choose their own seats and be comfortable: she did that just for us

Not forgetting Jackie Robinson the first black man to reach the Major leagues

And our First black President Barrack Obama, Are you still not yet intrigued?

Happy and proud to know that those women and men gave their lives for a reason

So we could shine today: this is our season

For if it was not for them, we could not be who we are

Singers, poets, doctors, actors and NBA Superstars!

Ok said the little boy, "Now I see"

Black History is the many African Americans who made a difference, and paved the way so I can be free.

STUDENTS POEMS ARE COOL

A poem can be fun a poem can be cool

Poems can teach you an important lesson or rule

Poems can make you laugh; they can even make you cry

A poem can make you smile and don't even know why

A poem can make you happy and do a cartwheel or a hand stand

A poem can make you mad and cause you to shout and fold your hands

A poem can make you dance all around the room

A poem can make you sad and fill your heart with gloom

But overall poems let others know how we feel

Poems are what you make them, that's what makes them real

TIME FOR KINDERGARTEN

Wake up mommy! It's time to go!

I am going to kindergarten didn't you know

I want to say my ABCs and count from one to ten

Sing songs, dress up and play pretend

Write my letters the best way I know how

Learn about animals like the horse, dog, and cow

I want to learn how to read and spell, how to have respect and treat others well

I want to learn about my Community Helpers

Like the doctor, nurse, mail man, and police officers

So come on mommy we can't be late!

I will love all my teachers, I think they will be great

CHILDREN NEVER FORGET YOU ARE SPECIAL

You are special, yes it is true

There is no one else in this world exactly just like you

There's no one else who smiles like you do

Cry, act, and laugh like you too

God took His time and formed each of your little parts

He made you all beautiful from the tip of your head right down to your hearts

He knew that you would bring joy to everyone you meet

He knew that you may be a bit difficult at times, but overall He knew that you would be sweet

A sweet little boy or girl who would one day become someone great

Anything you want to be; but wait

Never ever forget that you are special, tell yourself this each and everyday

When others say you are not, tell them "Go Away"!

I am special I am special this is what I Know

God made me for a special reason, and I will shine wherever I go

SCHOOL

Acrostic Poem

S- Is for studying when no one tells you too

C- Is for carefully listening to what your teachers tell you

H- Is for having the right attitude even when you fail a test

O- Is for overcoming and always trying your best

O- Is for the opportunity to get a good Education

L- Is for living a better life and using what you've learned: all that important information

STUDENTS CHERISH WHERE YOU LIVE ST. THOMAS

Acrostic Poem

S- Is for the sandy white beaches and the salty air

T- Is for the Tomean dialect heard everywhere

T- Is for Tourism our island's most important industry

H- Is for Haven sight and its beautiful scenery

O- Is for outstanding Educators who teach us what we know

M- Is for making that Virgin Islands' pride show wherever we go

A- Is for all kinds of dishes locally prepared, like fungi and fried fish

S- Is for stopping the violence and living in unity, every Virgin Islander's real wish

LET'S ALL GET ALONG

Why do we fight in class so much?

Teacher, why was it my bag that Suzie just touch

Teacher, Johnny stole my pencil case

And Carl just spit in my face

Mary called me a name and I didn't do her anything

How can teacher really teach with all this fussing and fighting?

But teacher, Billy just wrote on my back

Teacher somebody stole my snack

Is all this fighting good for me?

Does it help me to learn my ABCs?

Why can't we just get along and be friends?

Everyone will be much happier when the day ends

What if teacher came to school and fussed with you all day?

What would you do then? What would you say?

So next time you want to complain just sing a happy song

And remember instead of fighting it's much easier to get along

TEACH ME

Teach me Teacher because I want to learn

Sometimes I give you such a hard time, because your attention I want to earn

It's not always easy being a student, teacher please understand

Sometimes I am so afraid to raise my hand

I want to say teacher I did not understand what you just said

Sometimes I feel ashamed and just bow my head

The other children will laugh and call me a fool

Teacher I do want to learn that is why every day I am in school

So teacher please teach me all I need to know

Until on my own I must go

Teacher please never gives up on the students, though at times our bad behaviors make you sad

Or when we fail your test and make you disappointed or mad

Just continue to teach us, and one day you will see

That sitting in your classroom hearing you teach, was the best place for us to be

Printed in the United States
By Bookmasters